WHY DID CHEROKEES MOVE WEST?

And Other Questions about the Trail of Tears

Susan Bivin Aller

LERNER PUBLICATIONS COMPANY · MINNEAPOLIS

A Word about Language

English word usage, spelling, grammar, and punctuation have changed over the centuries. We have preserved original spellings and word usage in the quotations included in this book.

Lerner Publications Company
A division of Lerner Publishing Group, Inc.
241 First Avenue North
Minneapolis, MN 55401 U.S.A.

Website address: www.lernerbooks.com

Library of Congress Cataloging-in-Publication Data

Josephson, Judith Pinkerton.
    Why did Cherokees move west? And other questions about the Trail of Tears /
by Judith Pinkerton Josephson.
        p.   cm. — (Six questions of American history)
    Includes bibliographical references and index.
    ISBN 978–1–58013–668–6 (lib. bdg. : alk. paper)
    1. Trail of Tears, 1838–1839—Juvenile literature. 2. Cherokee Indians—
History—Juvenile literature. I. Title.
    E99.C5J67 2011
    975.004'97557—dc22   2009047196

Manufactured in the United States of America
1 – DP – 7/15/10

TABLE OF CONTENTS

THE SIX QUESTIONS HELP YOU DISCOVER THE FACTS!

INTRODUCTION

In October 1837, the crunch of footsteps on dried leaves echoed through wooded mountains in the southeastern United States. Under the watchful eyes of U.S. soldiers, a group of 365 Cherokees plodded along dirt trails and roads. The group's 1,000-mile (1,600-kilometer) journey would take them to the region covered by modern-day Oklahoma. There, these Native Americans had been promised a new place to live.

Men, women, and children walked westward, traveling 10 to 20 miles (16 to 32 km) a day. Pebbles and stones cut their bare feet. Sunlight flickered on their faces. A deep longing for home and fear about what lay ahead saddened their hearts.

As bitter winter cold set in, many fell ill, especially children. One officer kept detailed records. He wrote, "November 1, 1837: buried Duck's child this morning . . . made 19 miles [31 km] to day." Another day's entry read, "December 1, 1837: Issued corn & fodder, Bacon & corn meal, buried Oolanheta's child to day."

These Cherokees walked for three months before reaching their new home. Fifteen died along the way, eleven of them children. Most were under the age of two. This group went voluntarily. But beginning in 1838, the government forced all Cherokees to leave their homeland and follow the same route west to Oklahoma. Their journey came to be known as the Trail of Tears. The Cherokee people also called the journey the Trail Where They Cried. Who were the Cherokees?

K

ILLINOIS

MISSOURI

OHIO

KENTUCK

TENNESSEE
CHARLESTON

NO
CARO

CHATTANOOGA

SOUTH
CAROLINA

FORT
PAYNE
NEW ECHOTA

MISSISSIPPI

MISSISSIPPI RIVER

TENNESSEE RIVER

GEORGIA

TRAIL OF
TEARS
1837-1838

This portion of the Trail of Tears passes near Spencer, Tennessee.

In 1942 Robert Lindneux painted this image (right) of Cherokees riding horses westward on the Trail of Tears. In reality, most Cherokees had to walk the entire way.

3 1326 00450 4421

ONE BEFORE THE STRANGERS CAME

In the 1400s, European explorers discovered the vast North American continent. But long before the explorers arrived, millions of Native Americans lived there. The Cherokees lived in villages in the southern Appalachian Mountains. They called themselves *Tsa-lagi*, meaning the Principal (first or main) People.

mountains in eastern North America. The Appalachians run from the southeast corner of Canada to the southern United States.

Cherokees believed the Great Spirit (the creator) had given them their homeland to live in forever. According to legends, animal and nature spirits lived in the homeland too. With flapping wings, Great Buzzard had carved valleys rich with soil and rugged mountains—the Great Smokies. Uktena, the horned serpent, had scratched claw marks on the mountains' rock cliffs.

Hundreds of native herbs grew on the hillsides. Cherokee healers used the herbs to treat illnesses. The land also provided the Cherokees with food. Using hand tools, women grew corn, beans, squash, and sunflowers. All land was shared in common.

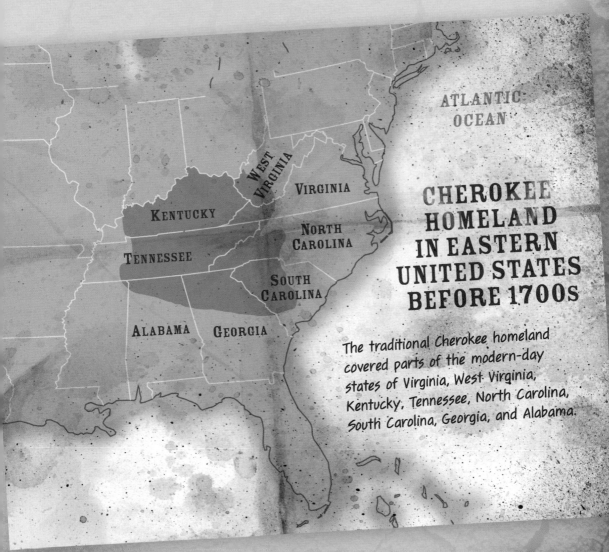

CHEROKEE HOMELAND IN EASTERN UNITED STATES BEFORE 1700s

The traditional Cherokee homeland covered parts of the modern-day states of Virginia, West Virginia, Kentucky, Tennessee, North Carolina, South Carolina, Georgia, and Alabama.

Above: Traditional Cherokee buildings still stand in Tennessee. *Right:* Cherokee farmers used hoes made of wood and stone to farm their fields.

Men helped clear land and harvest crops. But mainly, men were warriors, hunters, and fishers. They hunted white-tailed deer, wild turkeys, bears, rabbits, and squirrels. They killed animals only if they were needed for food or clothing.

Cherokee life was closely linked to the natural world and the seasons. Special ceremonies and dances marked each of the thirteen phases of the moon.

The year began with Cold Moon and ended with Snow Moon. In late summer, when the corn was almost ripe, villagers danced the Green Corn Dance ceremony. They shook rattles, chanted, and danced in lines.

Rivers crisscrossed Cherokee land. The Cherokees traveled on the rivers from village to village. They used canoes made from hollowed-out giant poplar trees.

MOON PHASES

Thirteen moon phases, each lasting about twenty-eight days, divided the Cherokee year. Each phase had a name: Cold Moon, Bone Moon, Wind Moon, Flower Moon, Planting Moon, Green Corn Moon, Ripe Corn Moon, End of Fruit Moon, Nut Moon, Harvest Moon, Hunting Moon, and Snow Moon.

To make dugout canoes (above), Cherokees burned and carved out the center of large tree trunks.

WHAT DID CHEROKEES WEAR?

For most of the year, Cherokees wore clothing made from soft deerskin. Women and girls dressed in skirts and ponchos. Men wore leggings and breechclouts—pieces of hide that hung from the waist. In winter people wore heavier clothes made from the skins of buffalo and bear.

People decorated their clothes with beads, porcupine quills, and feathers. They made jewelry from animal teeth, bones, and seeds. Girls and women wore their hair straight and long. Boys and men shaved or plucked the hair on their heads except for a bristly row on top. For battles, men painted their bodies with bright colors.

Scattered among numerous Cherokee villages were seven large families, or clans. The clans were called Bird, Wolf, Deer, Wild Potato, Long Hair, Blue, and Paint. Men and women from the same clan could not marry. When people from different clans fell in love, they gave each other special gifts. Then the newlyweds became part of the wife's mother's clan.

In each village, the largest and most important building was the council house. Inside the council house, a sacred fire always burned. People gathered around the fire to make important decisions. They also used the council house for ceremonies and dances.

Since ancient times, the Cherokees had lived this way. But when big ships carrying European explorers arrived, life changed. Countries such as Spain, Portugal, France, and England all wanted to claim this new world and its wealth of

In this 1988 painting by John Berkey, Spanish explorers meet with Cherokee Indians in the 1560s.

natural resources. Spanish explorers first met Cherokees in 1540 while searching for gold.

materials that occur naturally in an environment, such as soil, water, minerals, plants and trees, and animals

Objects new to the Cherokees came with the Europeans—brass kettles, metal hatchets, scissors, knives, woven material, trinkets, guns, and rifles. Native Americans traded deerskins, beeswax, and woven baskets for these goods. But bad things also arrived with the newcomers. The strangers brought serious diseases, such as measles and smallpox, that passed from person to person.

Many Cherokees and other Native Americans easily caught these serious diseases and died.

Cherokees tried to get along with the newcomers. But more and more European settlers were moving onto Indian land. Fighting broke out between the settlers and the Native Americans. To try to keep the peace, Cherokees signed treaties between 1721 and 1777 that gave up almost half of their hunting lands to white settlers.

> settlers
> people who come to live in a new region

> treaties
> agreements between two or more groups. Treaties often promise cooperation and an end to fighting.

During the Revolutionary War (1775–1783), American colonists fought Great Britain for their freedom. The colonists won and formed a new country, the United States of America. After that, settlers tried to take more Cherokee land in what later became the states of Georgia, Tennessee, Alabama, and North Carolina. The settlers killed Cherokees, burned their crops, and destroyed their villages.

The Cherokees were fierce warriors, and they fought back. Sometimes during attacks, Cherokee warriors scalped white Americans. Cherokees cut the scalp, with the hair attached, from a person's head. Usually the person died. If the person lived, he or she was scarred for life. White Americans viewed scalping as a savage act.

In 1785 the Cherokees signed the Treaty of Hopewell with the United States. The U.S. government promised not to settle on Cherokee land. But the promises were soon broken. To the Cherokees, the white man's words, written on paper

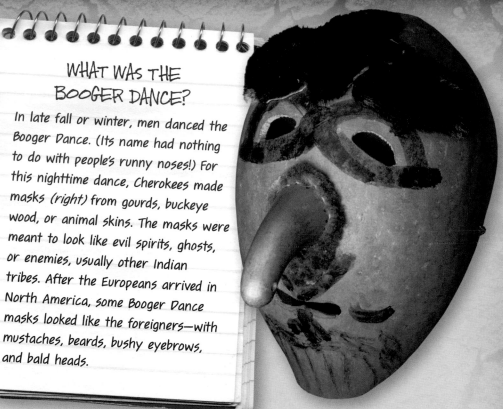

WHAT WAS THE BOOGER DANCE?

In late fall or winter, men danced the Booger Dance. (Its name had nothing to do with people's runny noses!) For this nighttime dance, Cherokees made masks (right) from gourds, buckeye wood, or animal skins. The masks were meant to look like evil spirits, ghosts, or enemies, usually other Indian tribes. After the Europeans arrived in North America, some Booger Dance masks looked like the foreigners—with mustaches, beards, bushy eyebrows, and bald heads.

that rustled, were "talking leaves." They blew away when no longer useful.

Vowing to stay united, Cherokees rebuilt their villages and replanted their fields. But many Americans still thought all Native Americans were savages.

NEXT QUESTION

WHAT COULD CHEROKEES DO TO LIVE PEACEFULLY AMONG THEIR FOREIGN NEIGHBORS?

TWO "CIVILIZING" THE CHEROKEE

Many Americans believed Native Americans should become "civilized." This meant living in European-style houses, wearing European clothing, changing their names, and becoming Christians.

In 1792 U.S. president George Washington sent federal agents to help civilize the Cherokees. With the agents came blacksmiths, millers, weavers, and other crafters. They brought plows, spinning wheels, and looms for weaving cloth.

President George Washington

Americans wanted to introduce European ways to Native Americans. Cherokee women learned to use spinning wheels *(left)* to make cloth.

Cherokee women were told that instead of farming, they should keep house and cook. They should sew gowns made from woven cloth, rather than animal skins. Many Cherokee women liked using the cloth, especially for diapers and washrags.

Men were taught to farm with plows and horses, not with simple tools. They were told to plant wheat along with corn. Instead of hunting, men raised sheep, cattle, goats, and horses.

A Cherokee's name had always described something special about the person. The woman's name Ayita means "first to dance." The man's name Tooantuh means "spring frog." Now Cherokees were encouraged to use Americanized names.

In schools run by Christian missionaries, teachers taught reading, writing, and arithmetic. Students also studied the Bible. Missionaries taught housekeeping, personal grooming, and table manners according to white traditions.

> **missionaries,** people who teach a new religion to native people. Missionaries in North America usually taught Christianity to Native Americans.

They said traditional Indian dancing, ball games, and hunting were wrong.

Some men and women refused to adapt to the new ways. In the 1790s, angry young Cherokee warriors became a problem on the frontier. They stole horses from white settlers. In revenge, settlers attacked innocent Native Americans.

frontier: the farthest edge of a settled territory

Cherokees needed to restore order within their tribe. So a tribal Council of Chiefs from the seven clans turned to Cherokee war leader Kahnungdclageh. Kahnungdclageh's name meant "One Who Goes on the Mountaintop." He was later called Major Ridge. The council asked Major Ridge to take charge of an Indian police force, called the Light Horse Guard.

Major Ridge

This map from 1803 shows the new U.S. territory bought by President Thomas Jefferson through the Louisiana Purchase.

In 1801 Thomas Jefferson became U.S. president. He wanted the United States to expand. The 1803 Louisiana Purchase doubled the country's size. Yet Jefferson wanted more land. His government agents pressured Native American tribes to sell their land. Between 1804 and 1806, Cherokees gave up huge pieces of land in Tennessee.

Some Cherokees volunteered to begin moving westward. Those who stayed in the East saw that they needed to band together to survive. In 1817 the seven clans formed a central government, the Cherokee Nation. New Echota in Georgia became the nation's capital city. An elected committee of leaders together with the Council of Chiefs made sure that the clans all followed the same laws.

WHERE IS NEW ECHOTA?

The former capital of the Cherokee Nation is a state historic site. It is located about 3.5 miles (5.5 km) north of Calhoun, Georgia.

In 1818 the U.S. government paid for two Cherokee cousins, John Ridge and Elias Boudinot, to go to school in Connecticut. John (whose Cherokee name Skatlelohski meant "yellow bird") was Major Ridge's son. Elias's Cherokee name was Gallegina, meaning "deer." Both cousins did well at the school.

While in Connecticut, the cousins fell in love with local white girls. John Ridge and Sarah Bird Northrup began a relationship. And Elias Boudinot fell in love with Harriet Gold. But marriages between people of different races were rare in white society. The cousins' romances made people angry. When Ridge married Northrup in 1824, people shouted insults at their wedding carriage. Later, when Boudinot married Gold, local school officials called their marriage a crime.

The young men brought their wives back home to Georgia to live with the Cherokees. The Ridge and Boudinot families were a little shocked at their sons' marriages to white women.

CHEROKEES AS SLAVE OWNERS

By the early 1800s, some Cherokees had grown wealthy from running trading posts, inns, and toll roads (roads that drivers pay to use). They also ran ferries, carrying horses and wagons across rivers. As they grew rich, many Cherokees became slave owners. Throughout the American South, black slaves were forced to work on large farms called plantations. Like white slave owners, Cherokees also bought black slaves to farm their fields. Cherokees such as Major Ridge were kind slave masters. But other Cherokees treated their slaves poorly.

But the couples were welcomed. Many other mixed-race couples had become part of the Cherokees tribe.

Elias Boudinot and John Ridge had worked hard and earned a fine education. But they found that they were still not accepted in white society. This experience told the cousins that keeping their Cherokee identity strong was important.

During the 1820s and 1830s, both men became leaders of the Cherokee Nation. They could speak and write English, which helped them talk with white Americans. Another rising young leader was John Ross. His Cherokee name was Guwisguwi, meaning "rare white bird." Ross's father was Scottish. His mother was Cherokee.

John Ross as a young man in 1838

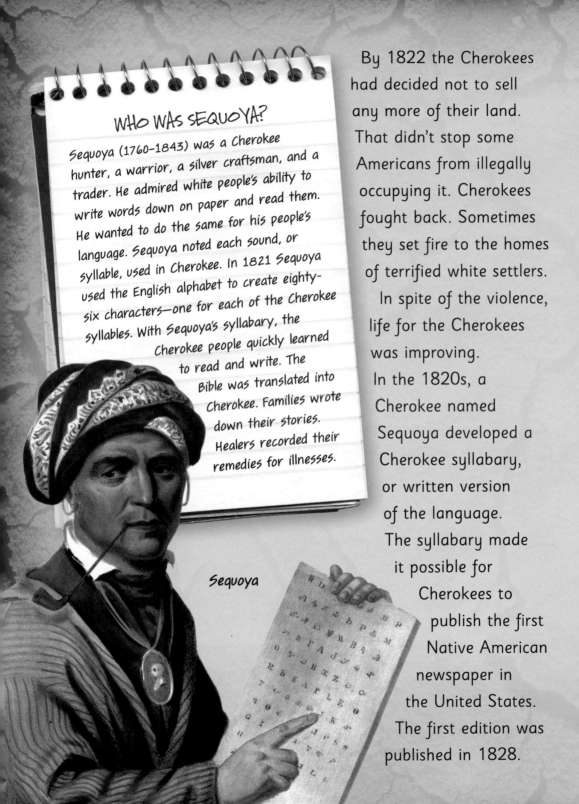

WHO WAS SEQUOYA?

Sequoya (1760–1843) was a Cherokee hunter, a warrior, a silver craftsman, and a trader. He admired white people's ability to write words down on paper and read them. He wanted to do the same for his people's language. Sequoya noted each sound, or syllable, used in Cherokee. In 1821 Sequoya used the English alphabet to create eighty-six characters—one for each of the Cherokee syllables. With Sequoya's syllabary, the Cherokee people quickly learned to read and write. The Bible was translated into Cherokee. Families wrote down their stories. Healers recorded their remedies for illnesses.

Sequoya

By 1822 the Cherokees had decided not to sell any more of their land. That didn't stop some Americans from illegally occupying it. Cherokees fought back. Sometimes they set fire to the homes of terrified white settlers.

In spite of the violence, life for the Cherokees was improving. In the 1820s, a Cherokee named Sequoya developed a Cherokee syllabary, or written version of the language. The syllabary made it possible for Cherokees to publish the first Native American newspaper in the United States. The first edition was published in 1828.

THE CHEROKEE CONSTITUTION

In 1827 Cherokee leaders wrote the government's first constitution. The document set clear land boundaries. It also named the nation's goals to "establish justice, promote our common welfare, and secure to ourselves and our posterity the blessings of liberty." These words were similar to ones in the preamble to the U.S. Constitution: "to promote the general Welfare, and secure the Blessings of Liberty to ourselves and our Posterity."

The newspaper was called the *Cherokee Phoenix* (*Tsa-la-gi Tsu-le-hi-sah-nuh-hi*). Printed in both English and Cherokee, the newspaper carried news and stories of culture and history. Elias Boudinot was the paper's first editor.

Efforts to civilize the Cherokees had made them stronger and wiser. The Cherokee word *currahee* (quu-wa-hi) means "stand alone." Pitted against settlers hungry for land and against the U.S. government, Cherokees stood alone. They had changed their ways to fit into white society. But nothing they did seemed to work.

NEXT QUESTION

WHAT WAS DISCOVERED ON CHEROKEE LAND IN 1829?

In this hand-colored woodcut, men search for gold in a Georgia stream. The discovery of gold on Cherokee land changed U.S. policies toward the Native Americans.

THREE A FATE SEALED

As the United States grew, white Americans debated what should be done about the Cherokees and other Native Americans. Many southerners felt that Native Americans, like black slaves, did not deserve the respect and rights that whites enjoyed. Some people wanted to move all Indians to a new territory west of the Mississippi River.

an area claimed by a government and subject to its laws

Not all white Americans thought this was a good idea. Respected politician Daniel Webster and well-known minister Jeremiah Everts argued against Indian removal. So did famous frontier explorer Davy Crockett.

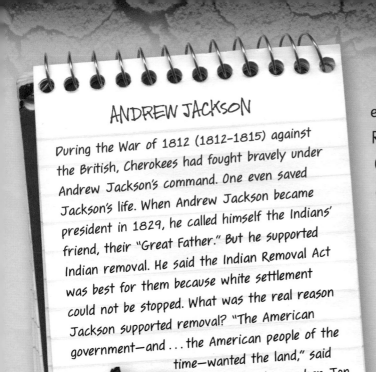

ANDREW JACKSON

During the War of 1812 (1812–1815) against the British, Cherokees had fought bravely under Andrew Jackson's command. One even saved Jackson's life. When Andrew Jackson became president in 1829, he called himself the Indians' friend, their "Great Father." But he supported Indian removal. He said the Indian Removal Act was best for them because white settlement could not be stopped. What was the real reason Jackson supported removal? "The American government—and . . . the American people of the time—wanted the land," said Jackson biographer Jon Meacham. "So they took it."

In 1828 thirty-eight-year-old John Ross became the Cherokees' principal chief. Soon after, in 1829, gold was discovered on Cherokee land in Georgia. This discovery made Cherokee land even more attractive to white settlers. Lawmakers in the U.S. Congress in Washington, D.C., argued for months about Indian removal. Then, on May 29, 1830, U.S. president Andrew Jackson signed the Indian Removal Act. The act would rid the eastern states of all Native American tribes.

President Andrew Jackson

How could the Cherokees fight the Indian Removal Act? People made suggestions, but no plan suited everyone. Chief Ross told his people to wait for the next election. A new president and a new Congress might think differently.

Other Cherokees did not believe things would improve. Each day brought new stories of Native Americans being beaten, run off their farms, and even killed by white Georgians. Leaders such as Major Ridge, John Ridge, and Elias Boudinot believed that Cherokees would be better off moving west.

"The clouds may gather, thunders roar, and lightning flash from the acts of [Georgia]... but the Cherokees with an honest patriotism and love of country will still remain peaceably and quietly in their own soil."
—Chief John Ross, July 24, 1830

Chief John Ross

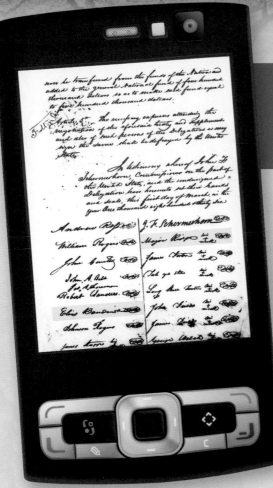

This is the final page of the Treaty of New Echota, including the signatures of Major Ridge and Elias Boudinot (highlighted).

On December 29, 1835, the U.S. government presented Cherokee leaders with the Treaty of New Echota. The treaty said that the tribe would give up their homeland within two years—by May 25, 1838. Cherokees would relocate to a territory in modern-day Oklahoma. The government promised to pay five million dollars to cover the loss of homes, schools, land, and the cost of the journey west.

Chief John Ross was against the treaty. But Major Ridge, John Ridge, Boudinot, and others agreed to the terms. The Ridges and Boudinot knew their group did not have the right to decide for the entire Cherokee Nation. They signed the treaty anyway, in early 1836.

Soon after, the Ridge and Boudinot families and about two thousand Cherokees left for the West. They joined the Cherokees who had volunteered to leave years before. The government had promised each volunteer "a good rifle, a blanket, a kettle, and five pounds of tobacco." Cherokees were also promised fifty dollars for every other Cherokee they brought with them.

WHY DID THEY SIGN?

Elias Boudinot and others believed that moving the Cherokee Nation westward would save their people. Removal from Georgia would keep the nation together. Boudinot believed it would also save the Cherokees from always being looked down on as "savages" by white Georgians. Boudinot's support for removal made other Cherokees very angry. They thought Boudinot was a traitor. Boudinot knew how angry others were. But he wrote, "We will make and sign this treaty. . . . We can die, but the great Cherokee Nation will be saved."

This is a portrait of Elias Boudinot as a young man.

Ross and sixteen thousand other Cherokees stayed behind. The removal deadline grew closer. In the spring of 1838, Ross sent a petition from house to house. The petition asked the U.S. Senate to think again about the removal decision.

Almost all remaining Cherokees signed the petition. But Congress ended its session (the time during which U.S. lawmakers meet in Washington, D.C.) before the petition arrived. The lawmakers never read it.

Ross struggled to hold his nation together. How long could the remaining Cherokees hold out?

NEXT QUESTION

HOW WOULD THE TREATY OF NEW ECHOTA CHANGE CHEROKEE LIVES?

U.S. soldiers in uniform and on horseback *(right)* oversee Cherokees on their way west during the removal in 1838.

_{FOUR}THE TRAIL WHERE THEY CRIED

The May 25, 1838, removal deadline finally came. The next morning, on May 26, U.S. troops appeared at Cherokee homes. A few kind soldiers allowed people to collect cooking utensils, some clothes, and blankets. Other soldiers pushed their captives empty-handed from their homes. Families left crops and livestock in the fields, family dogs barking, and meals on the table.

The Cherokees were first herded into thirty-one forts built near native villages. People huddled, cramped close together. Families had to claim small patches of space for their few belongings. Frightened children wandered about.

Foul smells rose from toilet pits. Next, the Cherokees were moved to prison camps. Diseases and sickness in the camps killed hundreds.

Then U.S. Army general Winfield Scott began the push westward. He loaded groups of Cherokees onto crowded flatboats to float down the Tennessee River. The situation on board shocked Christian missionary Daniel S. Butrick. Butrick later wrote, "Who would think of crowding men, women, and children, sick and well, into a boat together, with little, if any more room . . . than would be allowed to swine [pigs] taken to market?" When underwater sandbars or shallow water made it impossible for the flatboats to go on, the Cherokees had to walk.

boats with flat bottoms, used to travel in shallow water

Cherokees going west on the Trail of Tears traveled by foot. They crossed the Tennessee River on flatboats.

In early fall, Chief Ross convinced Scott to let Cherokees organize their own removal. Moving more than thirteen thousand people to a new location 1,000 miles (1,600 km) away was like moving an entire city. Ross and his brother Lewis divided people into thirteen groups of one thousand each. Each group had a leader, a doctor, an interpreter, a wagon master, and a Light Horse Guard of ten to twelve Cherokees.

Between late September and November 1838, all the organized groups headed westward. Each followed slightly different routes. Their journeys lasted three to six months.

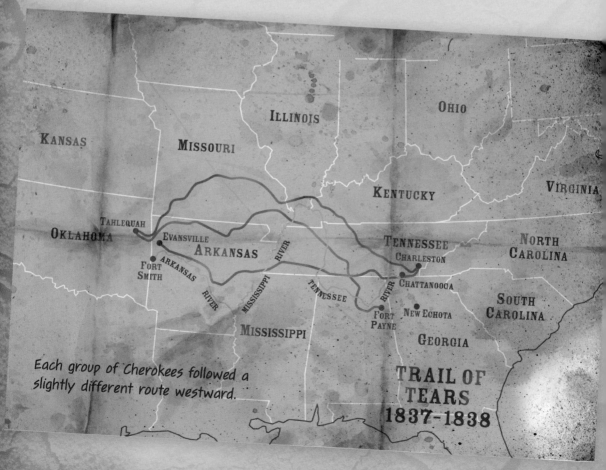

Each group of Cherokees followed a slightly different route westward.

TRAIL OF TEARS 1837-1838

Many who walked west did so with aching hearts. Their land had been home to many generations. The farther away they went, the less familiar were the smells of the forest, the tracks of animals, and the calls of birds.

The Cherokees plodded on through Alabama, Tennessee, and Mississippi. At times, they followed beaten paths through mountain passes. But in some places, marchers had to make their own path through thick forests.

FIVE CIVILIZED TRIBES

White settlers thought that five eastern Native American groups fit best with white society. Settlers called these groups the Five Civilized Tribes. Of these, the Cherokees were the most developed and literate (able to read and write). The other four groups were the Seminole, the Chickasaw, the Choctaw, and the Creek. The Indian Removal Act forced all five tribes to move westward. Like the Cherokees, these other Native Americans walked similar trails of tears.

The government had promised to pay $65.88 per person for the trip. That amount allowed for $.16 per person and $.40 per animal each day. The money covered food, wagons, and supplies. Travelers ground dried corn into flour. They ate pork cured in salt, and occasionally, they had beef. Horses and oxen ate huge amounts of the grain rations. Sometimes, families had to choose between feeding animals or feeding people.

In late fall, temperatures dropped. Dirt trails became rutted, frozen mud puddles. Only the elderly or those too ill to walk were allowed to ride in the wagons heaped with supplies.

A New England traveler said of one Cherokee group, "Two thousand people, sick and feeble, many near death. . . . [A great many] go on foot—even aged females . . . traveling with heavy burdens attached to the back . . . with no covering for the feet except what nature had given them."

"The Cherokee removal was the cruelest work I ever knew."
—A white Georgia volunteer soldier

One of the worst winters in history blustered in. By the time the Cherokees reached the Mississippi River, it had frozen into shifting sheets of ice. Snow and ice delayed some groups there for weeks. They sat and slept on the frozen ground until the weather improved. Few had clothing warm enough for the teeth-chattering cold.

The Cherokees had to press on even during the bitter cold, snow, and ice of winter. This 1992 painting is by Cherokee artist Troy Anderson.

The winter brought even more death. Tired, cold, and weak, Cherokees had no strength to fight diseases. Cholera and typhus (caused by drinking dirty, germ-filled water), measles, and lung and throat diseases killed many. Chief Ross's wife, Quatie, died of pneumonia (a lung infection) on the trail. Children and the elderly suffered the most. Shallow graves lined the route.

About four thousand Cherokees died on the Trail of Tears. Those who survived worried about the days ahead. They had lost their homeland. Would they ever return to their way of life?

THE CHEROKEE ROSE

Mothers of children who died on the Trail of Tears wept so bitterly that Cherokee leaders asked the Great Spirit to ease the mothers' suffering. A legend says that the Great Spirit answered the plea. From then on, wherever a mother's tears fell to the ground, a beautiful white rose grew. Georgia's state flower is the Cherokee Rose (below).

NEXT QUESTION

WHERE IN THIS STRANGE PLACE WOULD THE CHEROKEES MAKE A NEW START?

WHAT
WHERE
WHY
WHEN
HOW
WHO
WHAT
WHERE
WHY
WHEN
HOW
WHO
WHAT
WHERE
WHY
WHEN

In some parts of Oklahoma, the Cherokees found hot, dry prairies (below). This land was very different from their homeland in Georgia.

FIVE A NEW LIFE IN THE WEST

Each group of Cherokees arrived in Oklahoma exhausted and hungry. They had walked more than 1,000 miles (1,600 km), one-third of the way across North America.

At first, their new home looked similar to their former land. The steep, wooded hills might have been carved by the same Great Buzzard that made the rugged Smoky Mountains. Uktena, the great horned serpent, might have scratched claw marks on the rock cliffs, just as in the old country. Hope blossomed.

But as the Cherokees looked more closely, they saw that Oklahoma was not like their homeland. The soil was thin and scorched dry by heat. Huge swarms of grasshoppers ate the plants growing in fields. Rivers and streams often overflowed, and the floodwaters washed away crops.

The U.S. government had promised to supply food for one year—pork, beef, grain for flour, corn, and salt. But rations were not large enough to feed everyone. In some cases, supplies never arrived. In other cases, dishonest officials kept good supplies and handed out bad substitutes. They gave the Cherokees shriveled corncobs and old, scrawny cattle.

Many Cherokees blamed those who had signed the Treaty of New Echota for their people's troubles. They were very angry. On June 21, 1839, in Oklahoma some Cherokees murdered the leaders who had signed the treaty—Major Ridge, John Ridge, and Elias Boudinot. Many believed that justice had been done.

WHERE IS TAHLEQUAH, OKLAHOMA?
Tahlequah became the capital city of the Cherokees who moved to Oklahoma. It is in eastern Oklahoma, about 65 miles (105 km) southeast of Tulsa.

More conflicts arose. More than five thousand Cherokees who had relocated in the past twenty years were called the Old Settlers. They resented the thousands who had just arrived. People argued. Who should lead? Which laws would everyone follow?

John Ross wanted to heal the Cherokee Nation. In the fall of 1839, Ross helped all agree upon a constitution similar to the one written in 1827. But the disputes and violence continued. Finally, in 1846 the two groups—the newcomers and the Old Settlers—came together to form a newly reunited Cherokee Nation. They chose Tahlequah, Oklahoma, as their capital.

A painting by John Mix Stanley in 1843 shows a meeting of the tribes at Tahlequah, Oklahoma, called to work out differences among the groups of relocated Cherokees.

As the years passed, the hardships lessened. By 1860 the Cherokees had excellent schools. Businesses thrived. The population had doubled to twenty-one thousand. The people had adopted many modern ways. Yet they honored the old ceremonies, dances, and ancient traditions.

From 1861 to 1865, the United States fought the Civil War over states' rights and slavery. The Union soldiers from the North defeated Southern Confederate soldiers to win the war. The country was reunited. But for the Cherokees, an old problem soon arose. An endless stream of pioneers kept pushing westward.

THOSE WHO ESCAPED

U.S. soldiers did not succeed in rounding up all the Cherokees in 1838. Close to one thousand people escaped. They hid in the mountains or were sheltered by kind, white neighbors. Descendants of those Cherokees form part of the Eastern Band of Cherokee Indians in North Carolina.

This 1888 photograph shows a Cherokee family in front of their home in North Carolina. The family is descended from the Cherokees who stayed in the East.

It wasn't long before the U.S. government again told the Cherokees to give up land in their new location.

By this time, Chief Ross was in his seventies. Yet he and other Cherokee leaders traveled to Washington, D.C., to ask U.S. lawmakers to protect Cherokee rights. In 1865, while in Washington, Ross became seriously ill. He died on August 1, 1866.

In the late 1800s, the Cherokees were forced to sell even more land to white settlers. They had to give some land to other Native American groups that were also forced to

A group of seven delegates joined Chief Ross (not pictured) on his trip to Washington, D.C., in 1865. These five delegates (above) are the sons and grandsons of early Cherokee leaders John Ridge, Major Ridge, Stand Watie, and Elias Boudinot.

In 1893 the U.S. government decided that white settlers could claim Cherokee land in northern Oklahoma. That September about one hundred thousand white settlers rushed to the territory to grab plots of land *(above).*

move westward. And some Cherokee land was divided by newly built railroads.

In 1906 the U.S. government dissolved the Cherokee Nation. The next year, Oklahoma became a state. The Cherokees became citizens of the United States. The tribal government no longer led the Cherokee people.

Some Cherokees moved to cities and towns. But many Cherokees still worked to hold their communities together. In the 1970s, the U.S. government restored the Cherokee Nation's government. The Cherokees could again elect their own leaders.

The Cherokee Nation has also worked to preserve its history. Traditions, ceremonies, and stories from the Trail of Tears live on. They are passed from generation to generation. Gayle Ross, a descendant of John Ross, said, "In listening to the stories of your ancestors, you're taught who you are and what your ancestors sacrificed so that you could be Cherokee."

About 240,000 people are currently part of the Cherokee Nation in Oklahoma. Another Oklahoma group, the United Keetoowah Band of Cherokee Indians, has 10,000 members.

These Cherokees wear traditional dress at a Native American powwow in Maryland. Powwows are large meetings held throughout the country each year. Native Americans of many backgrounds gather at powows to celebrate their heritage.

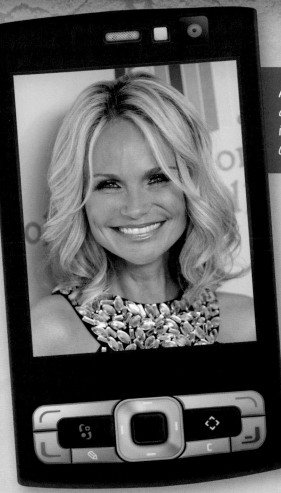

Actor Kristin Chenoweth has appeared in *Glee* and many other TV series and movies. She is one-quarter Cherokee. She was born in Oklahoma in 1968.

The Eastern Band of Cherokee Indians in North Carolina has about 13,500 members. Thousands of other Americans proudly claim Cherokee heritage—including actors Kristin Chenoweth, Wes Studi, and James Garner and movie director Quentin Tarantino. Another famous Cherokee is Wilma Mankiller, the first woman to be elected principal chief. She held that office from 1987 to 1995. Cherokees are part of the multicultural tapestry of America.

NEXT QUESTION

HOW DO WE KNOW WHAT HAPPENED ALONG THE TRAIL OF TEARS?

Primary Source: John G. Burnett's Report

The best way to see into the past and learn about any historical event is with primary sources. Primary sources are created near the time being studied. They include diaries, letters, newspaper articles, documents, speeches, personal papers, pamphlets, photos, paintings, and other items. They are made by people who have direct, firsthand knowledge of the event.

We've learned about the Trail of Tears from the letters and stories of the Cherokees who walked the trail and the white people who went with them. Private John G. Burnett was a young U.S. soldier when he guided one of the first groups of Cherokees. On his eightieth birthday in 1890, he recalled what he saw:

> I saw the helpless Cherokees arrested and dragged from their homes, and driven at the bayonet [a knife attached to a rifle] point into the stockades [the prison forts]. . . . I saw them loaded like cattle or sheep into six hundred and forty-five wagons and started toward the west. One can never forget the sadness and solemnity of that morning. . . . Many of these helpless people did not have blankets and many of them had been driven from home barefooted. . . . The trail of the exiles [people forced to leave their homes] was a trail of death. They had to sleep in the wagons and on the ground without fire. . . . I have known as many as twenty-two of them to die in one night of pneumonia due to ill treatment, cold, and exposure. . . . I did my best for them when they certainly did need a friend. . . . Murder is murder and somebody must answer, somebody must explain the streams of blood that flowed in the Indian country in the summer of 1838. Somebody must explain the four-thousand silent graves that mark the trail of the Cherokees to their exile.

WRITING EXERCISE

Pretend you are a Cherokee boy or girl living with your family in the 1830s. In school you've been told about President Andrew Jackson's plan to remove your people from their homes. You decide to write a letter to President Jackson. Be sure to explain who you are and how you feel about the president's removal policy.

WHAT is your name?

HOW old are you?

WHAT clan do you belong to?

WHERE do you live?

WHY do you agree or disagree with the removal policy?

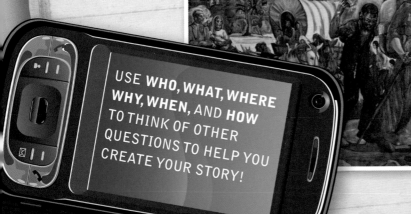

USE **WHO, WHAT, WHERE WHY, WHEN,** AND **HOW** TO THINK OF OTHER QUESTIONS TO HELP YOU CREATE YOUR STORY!

Timeline

1540

Spanish explorers first meet Cherokees while searching for gold.

1600s

English settlers arrive in North America.

1775–1783

American colonists fight Great Britain in the Revolutionary War. The colonists win and form the United States of America.

1785

The Treaty of Hopewell is signed.

1800

Washington, D.C., becomes the nation's capital.

1803

The Louisiana Purchase doubles the size of the United States.

1812–1815

The United States again fights and defeats Great Britain in the War of 1812.

1816–1830

Ohio, Indiana, Illinois, Tennessee, Mississippi, and Alabama become states.

1821

Sequoya creates a syllabary, a written Cherokee language.

1827

Cherokees write a constitution to govern their nation.

1828

Cherokees found the first Indian newspaper in America, the *Cherokee Phoenix*. John Ross is elected principal chief.

1829

Gold is discovered on Cherokee land in Georgia.

1830

Congress passes the Indian Removal Act.

1836

The U.S. government and some Cherokee leaders sign the Treaty of New Echota.

1838–1839

Cherokees are forced to walk westward on the **Trail of Tears.**

1839

Major Ridge, John Ridge, and Elias Boudinot are murdered by their own people.

1846

A reunited Cherokee Nation is established in Oklahoma.

1861–1865

Abraham Lincoln is president. The North fights the South in the U.S. Civil War. Black slavery ends.

1866

Principal Chief John Ross dies on August 1 at the age of seventy-five.

1906

The U.S. government dissolves the Cherokee Nation.

1907

Oklahoma gains statehood.

1976

Cherokees create a new constitution that restores the Cherokee Nation.

1987

Wilma Mankiller is elected principal chief of the Cherokee Nation.

Source Notes

4 Vicki Rozema, *Voices from the Trail of Tears* (Winston-Salem, NC: John F. Blair, 2003), 83.

4 Ibid., 88.

21 Theda Purdue and Michael D. Green, *The Cherokee Nation and the Trail of Tears* (New York: Viking, 2007), 40.

21 "Preamble," at *The United States Constitution Online*, 2010, http://www.usconstitution .net/const.html#Preamble (March 16, 2010).

23 Jon Meacham, *American Lion: Andrew Jackson in the White House* (New York: Random House: 2008), 93.

24 Purdue and Green, 69.

26 Purdue and Green, 118.

26 Elias Boudinot, *Cherokee Editor: The Writings of Elias Boudinot,* ed. Theda Perdue (Athens: University of Georgia Press, 1996), 27.

29 Rozema, 141.

32 PBS, "The Trail of Tears" in *We Shall Remain*, transcript, April 27, 2009, http://www .pbs.org/wgbh/amex/weshallremain/files/transcripts/WeShallRemain_3_transcript.pdf, 13 (March 16, 2010).

32 Meacham, 318.

40 PBS, "The Trail of Tears," 14.

42 Thomas Bryan Underwood, *Cherokee Legends and the Trail of Tears: From the Nineteenth Annual Report of the Bureau of American Ethnology* (Washington, DC: Smithsonian Institute, 1956), 21–27.

Selected Bibliography

Golden Ink. "Major Ridge." About North Georgia. 2010. http://ngeorgia.com/ang/ Major_Ridge (February 26, 2010).

Ehle, John. *Trail of Tears*. New York: Anchor Books, 1988.

Meacham, Jon. *American Lion: Andrew Jackson in the White House*. New York, Random House, 2008.

Mooney, James. *Myths of the Cherokee*. New York: Dover Publications, 1995.

Museum of the Cherokee Indian. N.d. http://www.cherokeemuseum.org (February 26, 2010).

Purdue, Theda, and Michael D. Green. *The Cherokee Nation and the Trail of Tears*. New York: Viking, 2007.

Rozema, Vicki. *Voices from the Trail of Tears*. Winston-Salem, NC: John F. Blair, 2003.

Further Reading and Websites

Behrman, Carol H. *Andrew Jackson*. Minneapolis: Lerner Publications, 2005. Learn about the life and career of the seventh U.S. president.

Broyles, Anne, and Anna Alter. *Priscilla and the Hollyhocks*. Watertown, MA: Charlesbridge, 2008. Learn what life was like for an African American slave owned by a Cherokee family and what happens to her when she walks the Trail of Tears.

Cherokee Indian Fact Sheet
http://www.bigorrin.org/cherokee_kids.htm
Read all sorts of facts about Cherokee culture and history.

Corneilissen, Cornelia. *Soft Rain: A Story of the Cherokee Trail of Tears*. New York: Yearling, 1999. A Cherokee girl experiences the hardships of 1838 leading up to and including the journey along the Trail of Tears.

Levine, Michelle. *The Cherokees*. Minneapolis: Lerner Publications Company, 2007. Levine details the history, the traditions, and the modern-life of Cherokees. Other books in the Native American Histories series include *The Seminoles, The Chocktaws,* and *The Creek*.

Native Languages of the Americas: Cherokee (Tsalagi)
http://www.native-languages.org/cherokee.htm
Find out the names of animals and other words in the Cherokee language.

Penn, Audrey. T*he Whistling Tree*. Washington, DC: Child & Family Press, 2003. Follow a modern-day Cherokee girl as she learns more about her heritage and the stories of her people.

Roop, Peter, and Connie Roop. *If You Lived with the Cherokee*. New York: Scholastic, 1998. Peek back into time to learn what life was like in Cherokee villages and how life changed for the people after the Trail of Tears.

Smith, Cynthia Leitich. *Indian Shoes*. New York: HarperCollins, 2002. Read about a modern-day Cherokee boy living with his grandfather in Chicago.

Waxman, Laura Hamilton. *Sequoyah*. Minneapolis: Lerner Publications, 2004. Waxman details the life of the famous Cherokee leader and inventor of the Cherokee syllabary.

Index

Photo Acknowledgments

The images in this book are used with the permission of: © iStockphoto.com/DNY59, p. 1; © Photodisc/Getty Images, pp. 1 (background) and all cracked mud backgrounds; © iStockphoto.com/sx70, pp. 3 (top), 9 (top), 10, 13 (top left), 16 (top), 19 (top), 20 (top), 21 (top), 23 (top), 26 (left), 31, 33 (top), 37 (top); © iStockphoto.com/Ayse Nazli Deliormanli, pp. 3 (bottom), 43 (left); © iStockphoto.com/Serdar Yagci, pp. 4–5 (background), 43 (background); © Bill Hauser/Independent Picture Service, pp. 4–5, 7, 18 (inset), 30, 35 (inset); © iStockphoto.com/Andrey Pustovoy, pp. 5 (top), 8 (bottom), 15, 25, 41 (top); © Phil Schermeister/National Geographic/Getty Images, p. 5 (inset); The Granger Collection, New York, pp. 5 (bottom), 29, 39; © Stock Connection/SuperStock, p. 6; © Marilyn Angel Wynn/Nativestock.com, pp. 8 (top & inset), 9, 32, 45; © John Berkey/National Geographic/Getty Images, p. 11; © Richard A. Cooke/CORBIS, p. 13 (top right); Tennessee State Museum Collection, p. 14 (top); Library of Congress, pp. 14 (bottom, LC-DIG-pga-01368), 16 (bottom, LC-USZC4-3158), 20 (bottom, LC-USZC4-4815), 23 (bottom, LC-USZC4-6466); © Danny Lehman/Terra/CORBIS, p. 15 (inset); © North Wind Picture Archives, pp. 17, 22; © iStockphoto.com/Talshiar, pp. 18, 35; © MPI/Archive Photos/Getty Images, pp. 19 (bottom), 24; National Archives, p. 25 (inset); Research Division of the Oklahoma Historical Society, p. 26 (right); Collection of the State Museum of Oklahoma, Oklahoma Historical Society, pp. 28, 43 (middle); © Steffen Hauser/Alamy, p. 33 (middle); © Dan Van Den Broeke/Dreamstime.com, p. 34; © Smithsonian American Art Museum, Washington, DC/Art Resource, NY, p. 36; Rue des Archives/The Granger Collection, New York, p. 37 (bottom); © Apic/Hulton Archive/Getty Images, p. 38; © Tom Carter/Alamy, p. 40; AP Photo/Evan Agostini, p. 41 (inset); © SuperStock/SuperStock, p. 44.

Front cover: The Granger Collection, New York. Back cover: © Photodisc/Getty Images (background).